JAVA

Basic Fundamental Guide for Beginners

TABLE OF CONTENTS

Introduction

Congratulations and thank you for downloading *Java*.

Only a few languages have redefined the way of programming like Java has. Every year, the Java language keeps changing and evolving. One reason to explain this was the culture of innovation and the need for change to fulfill a given desire.

Java comprises of a compiler, Java virtual machine (JVM), libraries, and the language itself. The Java virtual machine is responsible for allowing software developers from different platforms to write code in different languages which will still be executed on the JVM. The design of the Java language was on the basis of the following features:

- Independence of a platform.

- A language which is strongly typed

- An automatic memory management

- An object-oriented language

- A language which is interpreted and compiled.

In this eBook, you will learn and practice the important concepts of the Java programming language. You will learn about the classes, methods and inheritance and many other basic concepts about the Java language. This eBook will help you develop Java programming skills important to start solving real-world problems. You will learn the fundamentals of the Java language and how you can use them in your program. Java is a very popular language and easy to learn. It is a widely used language to develop android apps and web applications. If you are new to programming and want to gain the fundamentals concepts in Java, reading this book will prove a valuable choice for you.

Chapter 1

Java Fundamentals

Java Program and its Development Environment

The invention of the Internet alongside with the World Wide Web redefined the computing sector. Before the advent of the internet, the cyber industry was driven by the stand-alone PCs. Nowadays, about every computer is connected to the internet. The internet has been redefined to the point where it allows the sharing of files and information across multiple devices. Today, it has grown and expanded widely. So, with the above changes. We had new ways which you can code in Java.

Java is a special language which is mostly used on the internet. But, that is not enough. There are so many things which it can help one accomplish. However, it is more than that. We can say that Java redefined the programming sector, it revolutionized the way programmers can think about its function and structure. To become an expert in Java language, you need to do a lot of practice in coding. This chapter will take you through some of the Java fundamentals, we shall teach you the history of Java and some of its important features.

One of the most interesting things about learning to program in any language whether it is python, PHP, etc. is that no element exists on its own. Rather, every component of the language works hand-in-hand with another component. This kind of relationship is dominant in Java. For your information, every time you want to discuss a given concept in Java, most of the time you may need to involve another related topic. This is something that you are going to realize as a means to solve such a problem. We shall give you a briefing about the features of Java programming in this Chapter including a simple Java program.

We shall not dig deep into the details, but we shall focus on the general concepts which are prominent in any Java program.

How Java Started

I know this is something which you would like to know especially if you are just starting out in Java programming. It is important as a new beginner to Java programming to know its origin because everything has its place of origin. Well, you need to know that there are two factors which contribute to language innovation in the computing industry. These two factors include enhancement in the way we program and the modifications in the computing environment. Java is founded based on these two factors. It is built upon the existing foundation of the C and C++ programming languages. In other words, Java improves on the overall aspects of the two programming languages. As a response to the alarming rise of the online presence, the language comes with several features to enhance the level of coding.

Would you want to know the people who invented Java? Of course, you do. James Gosling, Ed Frank, Mike Sheridan, Chris Warth, and Patrick Naughton at Sun Microsystems are behind the invention of the Java language in 1991. Before it was called Java, it was initially referred to as "Oak." The reason behind the invention of Java wasn't the internet, but instead, they wanted a language which could work on many different platforms to help in the creation of software. This software would later be installed in various consumer electronics. As you know, different CPUs types act as computer controllers. The major difficulty was, at that time, the majority of the languages used to program were meant to work on a specific device. For example, C++.

While you could compile a program in C++ for whatever CPU, to achieve this you had to have a complete C++ compiler designed for that specific CPU. The problem has been that compilers are very expensive. Besides that, they are time-consuming to develop. Therefore, in a move to find a much better solution to this problem,

James Gosling and his company decided to create a language which was cross-platform and portable. This would then make it possible to run on different CPUs under various environments. It was this effort which resulted in the release of Java.

Coincidentally, while Java was being created, something very important emerged. Later on, it came to be an important factor in the rise of Java programming. Had it not been for the World Wide Web, Java won't have become a very popular programming language applied in consumer electronics. But, the World Wide Web played a key role in the spread of Java programming because Java was a portable language and the Web required programs which were portable.

As a programmer, you have read several programming books or have heard your fellow programmer emphasize the importance of portable programs. Although the demand to have portable programs was an old idea, with the coming of the World Wide Web, this old problem re-emerged in a different manner. The members of the Java design experienced problems with portability. As you can guess, this discovery was what led the design team to shift their attention from the consumer devices to the Internet. In brief, the internet was the sole success for Java program.

Class Libraries in Java

In Java programming, we have something called class and method. We shall discuss this more in the coming Chapter. So, it is possible to create each method and class to have your Java programs. However, programmers in Java most of the time make use of the existing collection of methods and classes in the Java libraries. These are also known as the Java APIs.

We now want to look at the steps taken to create and execute an application in Java with the help of a Java development environment.

To begin with, Java programs usually go through a number of stages. There are five stages involved:

- Edit

- Compile

- Load

- Verify

- Execute

Something else I would want to mention is that you need to have installed the Java environment to help you run the program in Java. That is the JDK on your computer. The JDK is freely provided on the Oracle website.

There are several versions of JDK. Look and choose whichever fits your computer and operating system. Don't forget that the JDK runs in the command prompt platform and makes use of the command-line tools. In addition, there are several IDEs which you can use to run your Java programs. Some of them include Eclipse and NetBeans. Which to choose is up to your choice. Personally, I have worked with NetBeans.

If you visit the main Oracle website, you will read guidelines to help you install JDK on different operating systems.

However, let's assume that you are not using any of the above OS. I will suggest that you take time and read the documentation designed for the Java environment. Or you can find an instructor to help you out.

Creating a Program with Java

The first program comprises of doing a few edits to a program using the editor program. Most people call it an editor. You will use the editor to write your program and perform several changes. Java programs are saved with the name of the file which will end with the

.java. This shows that the file's source code uses the Java programming language.

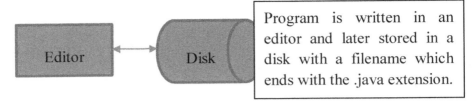

Program is written in an editor and later stored in a disk with a filename which ends with the .java extension.

Compile a Java program into Bytecodes

Now, in the second stage, the command Javac is used to compile the program. For example, if you want to run a Java program Firstprogram.java, then you must type:

Javac Firstprogram.java into the command window of your computer. In this case, the Command Prompt if you are working on Windows and the shell prompt if you are using Linux. For those using the Mac computers, you can use the Terminal application. If the program compilation succeeds, the compiler will produce a class file called Firstprogram.class.

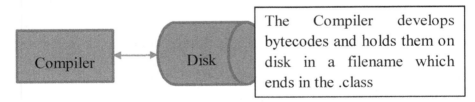

The Compiler develops bytecodes and holds them on disk in a filename which ends in the .class

The Compiler in Java will translate the source code into bytecodes which consist of the operations to be performed in the execution phase. The bytecodes are then executed in the Java Virtual Machine which is part of the JDK and the foundation of the Java platform. The Java Virtual Machine has been widely used as a virtual machine. The Microsoft's .NET applies the same virtual-machine architecture.

Now, unlike the machine language which relies on certain computer hardware, the byte-codes are independent. In other words, byte-codes don't rely on a specific hardware platform. Therefore, the bytecodes of Java are portable. This means that even if you don't recompile the source code, you can still execute the byte-codes on a different platform which has the JVM and can interpret the version of Java which the bytecodes are compiled.

Load a program into Memory

The virtual machine in Java will load the program for execution. This process is called loading. The class loader of the JVM has the .class files which contain the program's bytecodes and places them in the primary memory. The class loader will also load the .class files produced by the Java program. The .class files can be transferred from the disk on your system over a network.

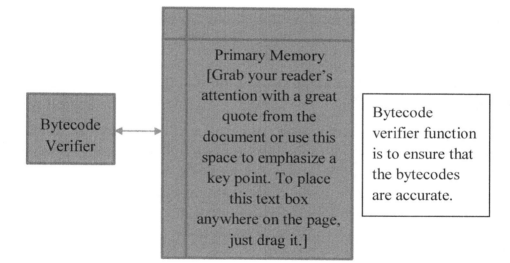

Execution Phase

The last phase is the execution phase. Here, the JVM has the role to execute the program's bytecodes. In other words, it will be executing problems detailed in the program. The early Java versions, the JVM acted as an interpreter for Java bytecodes. This resulted in slow execution in the majority of the Java programs. The slow execution was as a result of the JVM's need to interpret and execute a single bytecode at a time. However, we have modern computers which can execute different instructions in parallel. In fact, the modern JVMs can execute bytecodes by applying a combination of interpretation and the just-in-time compilation. This process involves the JVM performing bytecodes analysis when they are interpreted and look for hot spots parts in the bytecodes which execute regularly. In such cases, the just-in-time compiler will convert the byte-codes into computer's machine language. So, the next time the JVM comes in contact with the compiled parts, the faster machine language executes. Therefore, programs in Java run through two phases of compilation:

1. The source code is converted into bytecodes for the sake of portability across JVMs.

2. At the time of execution, the bytecodes are converted into machine language for the actual device which the program executes.

Some of the problems that might happen during the execution time

There are times when programs don't work on the first run. Each of the phases discussed above can fail because of some errors. For instance, a program which is in the process of execution might try to perform a division by zero. This would lead to the Java program to show an error message. If such a problem happens, you will need to go back to the editing phase and make the required corrections. Once you have done the corrections, you can proceed to the next phase to figure out whether the errors have been fixed.

Your first Java program

So far you have learned on the phases of creating, compiling and executing your Java program. We want to apply the knowledge in creating a simple Java program which prints a short message on your computer screen.

Here is the program you are going to learn how to write:

Example 1: Display message on computer screen.

```
class First {
  public static void main(String[] arguments) {
    System.out.println("Let's do something using Java technology.");
  }
}
```

You will type the above program in your favorite Java IDE. Once you have this program in your editor, it is time to compile and run it. The output should resemble the image below:

Output of program:

Let's briefly examine the components of the above program:

class First {

This line starts with the keyword *class* as a way to declare the class which is being defined. Class in Java represents the basic unit. In this example, *First* is the class name. Classes in Java begin with { and close with }. Whatever is found inside the curly brace belongs to class members. For now, don't be anxious about the class members, we shall handle that later.

public static void main (String args[]) {

9

In the code above, we have the *main()* method. All Java programs have the main function. We shall not explain in detail the meaning of the above line because you need to understand other features of Java first. But, because you are going to interact with the majority of the code in Java which uses this approach, we shall look at it in brief.

The name *public* is a keyword access modifier. This means that it determines the way the rest of the other programs will access the members in the class. In Java programming, if you have your class defined with the *public* keyword, members of the class are free to be used by the rest of the code in the program. However, this does not apply to a *private* class. As the name suggests, *private* classes have some restrictions.

The *String args []* are parameters of the main method. To relay information to the main method, we make use of it. In case a method does not have parameters, we use the empty parentheses.

The next line of the code,

System.out.println("Let's do something using Java technology".);

This line displays the details of the message you would like to print on the screen. The *println()* method is a built-in method. It always displays a string passed into it. Something you need to note is that the lines of code always end with a semicolon. The semicolon indicates the end of one line of Java code.

Chapter 2

Introduction to Java Operators
and Data Types

The main stem of a computer language is the aspect of the data types and operators. Java is not an exception to this. If you are starting out in Java programming, you must know the data types and operators in Java. These are the aspects which determine the limit of the language as well as which types of tasks it can perform. Luckily, there is an extensive list of operators and data types in Java. They help one program different types of problems.

As you will realize, data types and operators are an extensive topic. Therefore, we shall only look at the commonly used data types and operators in Java. We shall also discuss something to do with the variables and expression in Java.

Importance of Data Types

You might be wondering if it is important to discuss data types in Java programming. Well, here is the answer for you: Yes, it is. Why? Java is a strongly typed language. If there are any illegal operations, it won't be compiled. Therefore, this strong typing is important because it helps prevent errors and improves readability. For the strong typing to be successful, all variables, values, and expressions must have a specific type.

Primitive Type in Java

Built-in data types exist in two types:

- The one which is object-oriented

- The other one which is non-object-oriented

The object-oriented data types in Java are defined by classes. We shall discuss more on classes in the later chapters. At the foundation of Java, there were eight primitives used to demonstrate that these types are non-object-oriented. They were simply normal binary values. One of the reasons why they are not object-oriented is because of issues with efficiency. The following figure shows Java primitive types:

Type	Meaning
boolean	Represents true/false values
byte	8-bit integer
char	Character
double	Double-precision floating point
float	Single-precision floating point
int	Integer
long	Long integer
short	Short integer

Java provides a strict specification of the range and attributes of the primitive type. In all those specifications, the Java Virtual Machine has to support them. As a result of the portability aspect, Java cannot be compromised. For instance, an *int* will be the same for all environments. This makes programs be completely portable. It eliminates the requirement to rewrite the code so that it fulfills a given platform.

Integers

Integers in Java are of four types: *short*, *long*, *int*, and *byte*

Type	Width in Bits	Range
byte	8	−128 to 127
short	16	−32,768 to 32,767
int	32	−2,147,483,648 to 2,147,483,647
long	64	−9,223,372,036,854,775,808 to 9,223,372,036,854,775,807

As you will notice in the above table, the integers have been signed. In Java, it does not provide for unsigned integers. Majority of languages have unsigned and signed integers. The designers behind the Java language felt this was going to be unnecessary.

N/B

The Java runtime has the ability to make use of whichever size to contain the primitive. However, most of the time, the types should behave according to the way they have been outlined. The most common used integer in Java is the *int*.

When we have an integer whose range is beyond the *int*, we use the *long*. For example, if we have a program which computes a result such as 5280 * 13

The result of this operation can't be stored in an *int* variable. We use a long integer type. The smallest type of integer is the byte. Bytes are excellent when you have data in binary form. The short type often creates the short integer. Short variables are excellent when you don't want bigger values you get from *int*.

Floating point types

The floating type represents fractional numbers. The floating types exist in two types, the double and float. The double represents the double precision numbers while the float represents the single precision numbers.

The double is applied frequently since functions of mathematics use double value. For instance, sqrt() will output a double. You can check its application in the code below. In this example, sqrt() has been applied to calculate the longest side of a triangle when the length of the other sides has been provided.

```
/*
    Use the Pythagorean theorem to
    find the length of the hypotenuse
    given the lengths of the two opposing
    sides.
*/
class Hypot {
  public static void main(String args[]) {
    double x, y, z;

    x = 3;
    y = 4;                    Notice how sqrt( ) is called. It is preceded by
                              the name of the class of which it is a member.
    z = Math.sqrt(x*x + y*y);

    System.out.println("Hypotenuse is " +z);
  }
}
```

The output from the program is shown here:

```
Hypotenuse is 5.0
```

We need to notice in the example above that *sqrt()* belongs to the *Math* class. But, notice the way the *sqrt()* has been used: first, it has been preceded by the *Math* name. If you can recall the example we used in the first Java program in Chapter 1, we used *System.out* before the *println()* method. Now, for *sqrt()*, it is similar.

14

Characters

If you have programmed in another language, you might be thinking that characters in Java are 8. No! Java has Unicode. What a Unicode does is to define a set of characters which represents characters existing in the human languages. The example below demonstrates:

Char th;

th = 'Y';

Still, if you want to display a char value by applying the *println()* statement. This example will show you how to do it:

```
System.out.println("This is th: "+ th);
```
Given that the char is unsigned 16-bit type, you can do some arithmetic operations in the char variable. For instance, look at the program below:

```
Class CharArith {
Public static void main (String args []) {
Char th;
th = 'X';
System.out.println("th has "+ th);
th++; // we increment the th, it is possible to increment a char
System.out.println("th is now "+ th);
th = 90; // we assign th the value Z
System.out.println("th is now "+ th);
}
}
```
Here is the output of the above program:
```
"th has X"
"th is now Y"
"th is now Z"
```

This program assigns variable *th* the value *'X'*. Then, it is incremented to *Y*, which is the next character in the Unicode sequence.

The Boolean Type

In Java, the Boolean type refers to false or true values. Java finds out if it is true or false using the reserved keywords. Therefore, an expression Boolean type will assume one of these values. An example to demonstrate include:

15

```
class BoolPro {
public static void main (String args []) {
 boolean q;
q = false;
System.out.println ("q is "+ q);
q= true;
System.out.println("q is "+ q);
// a boolean value can also control the if statement
If(q)
System.out.println("This is executed.");
q = false;
if(q)
System.out.println("This is not executed");
// Describe the results of the relational operator
System.out.println("11 > 8 is "+ (10 > 8));
}
}
```
The output:
 q is false
q is true
This is executed
11 > 8 is true

There are a few things to note about this program. First, the *println()*, displays a boolean value. Secondly, the boolean values control the flow of an if statement. You don't need to go the long way in writing the boolean type this way: *if (b == true)*

The result shown by the operator such as < is boolean. It is one of the reasons why we have the expression *11 > 8* showing the value *true*. In addition, the other pair of parentheses near the *11 > 8* is important since plus comes before the >.

Literals

When it comes to literals in Java, we mean the fixed values which appear in the form in which human beings can read. We can say the number 200 is a literal. Most of the time, literals can be constants. Literals are important in a program. In fact, most Java programs use literals. Some of the programs we have already discussed in this book use literals.

Literals in Java can fall on various primitive data types. The manner in which every literal is shown is determined by its type. Like it was mentioned some time back, we enclose character constants in single quotes such as *'c'* and *'%'*.

We define literals in integers without involving the fractional part. For instance, 12 and -30 are integer literals. A floating point literal should contain the decimal point plus the fractional part. 12.389 is a floating literal. Java further permits for one to apply the scientific notation for the floating point literals. Integer literals contain int value and anyone can initialize them with a variable of *short, byte,* and *char*.

Hexadecimal, Binary, and Octal literals

A base-8 number system is octal, and it has 0 to 7 digits. In the octal number system, 10 is equivalent to 8 in decimal. The 16-base number system is referred to as hexadecimal and has the digits running from 0 to 9 together with the letters A to F.

Character Escape Sequences

Surrounding them with single quotes works for the majority of printing characters. However, there are certain characters which have a problem with the text editor. Furthermore, double and single quotes tend to have a unique meaning to Java. This means you cannot just use them directly. Now, because of the above reason, Java has specific escape sequences, sometimes it is called a *backslash character constant*. This table illustrates:

Escape Sequence	Description
\'	Single quote
\"	Double quote
\\	Backslash
\r	Carriage return
\n	New line
\f	Form feed
\t	Horizontal tab
\b	Backspace
\ddd	Octal constant (where ddd is an octal constant)
\uxxxx	Hexadecimal constant (where xxxx is a hexadecimal constant)

For example, *th* is assigned the tab character below:

```
th = '\t';
```
Next example, we assign a single quote to th
Th = '\' ';

String Literals

Java further supports other types of literal such as the string. These characters lie inside the double quotes. Take for example:

"come here" is a string. In the preceding Java programs, you must come across *println()* method. Besides the normal characters, it is possible for the string literal to have more than one escape sequences. Here is an example of what I am talking about,

```
// Demonstrate escape sequences in strings.
class StrDemo {
  public static void main(String args[]) {
    System.out.println("First line\nSecond line");
    System.out.println("A\tB\tC");
    System.out.println("D\tB\tF") ;
  }
}
```

Use \n to generate a new line.

Use tabs to align output.

The output is shown here:

```
First line
Second line
A          B          C
D          E          F
```

You should be able to recognize the \n escape sequence which has been applied in creating a new line. It is not a must to use the *println()* statements to receive the multiline output. You can get it by embedding the \n in the longer string where you want the new lines to appear.

Let's turn to variables

Variables in Java are declared using this syntax:

> *Type var-name;*

A variable can be declared of any type. This also includes the simple types and each variable will have a type. In other words, what a variable can do will be resolved by its type. For instance, a variable of *boolean* type can never be applied in storing a floating point value. In addition, the type of variable remains throughout its lifetime. For example, a floating variable will forever remain a floating variable. At no point will it change to become an int variable or character variable.

You need to also know that variable declaration is done before you can proceed to use it. This is crucial since the compiler has to know the data types which a variable contains before it does the compilation of a statement applied by the variable. This will also enhance strict type checking.

19

Variable Initializing

At a certain point in this chapter, I mentioned something about initializing. Well, if you didn't understand what I meant by variable initialization, it's time to understand. Generally, it is a requirement to have your variable store some value before we can use them. One of the easiest ways you can ensure that your variable has some value is using the assignment statement, which I believe you have seen in some examples. Another way you can do it is by assigning your variable an initial name before you proceed to use it. To achieve this, you use the equal sign and the value you would like to assign to the variable. In general, the syntax to follow for variable initialization is:

Type var = value;

In this, the value represents the value you would like to assign to the variable at the time of creation. It is important for the value to be compatible with the type of variable. You can look at some examples below:

int Sum = 12;

char th = 'T';

float f = 3.2 F // f has been initialized with the 3.2

Whenever you are declaring more than two variables of the same type by separating them with a comma, it is important to assign one with an initial value. Here is an example,

int x, y = 8, c = 11, d; // Y and c have been initialized with some values

Dynamic initialization

While in the previous examples, we have only made use of the constants in the initialization, Java will permit variable initialization dynamically on any valid expression at the time of declaration. For example,

You can have a look at this program which will calculate the volume of a cylinder when the radius and base have been provided:

```
Class DymVolume {
Public static void main (String args []) {
Double radius = 4, height 5;
double volume = 3.1416 * radius * radius * height;
System.out.println("Volume is "+ volume);
}
}
```

The scope and variable lifetime

So far, you have realized that all variable declaration happens at the main method when it starts.

However, Java will allow variable declaration in any block. A block will define the variable scope. In other words, when a new block begins, a new scope is created. A scope defines objects which will be accessible by the program. It also defines the lifetime of objects.

If it is not your first time to learn a computer language, then you must have come across other computer programming languages which tend to define two type of scopes, the global and local. While they are still supported in Java, this is not the right way to categorize scope in Java. The main scopes in Java as you will see are the ones defined by both the method and class.

In general, variables which have been declared within the scope aren't visible to the code which has been defined beyond the limits of the scope. Now, whenever you define a variable within a scope, you make that variable available as a local variable and safeguard it against unauthorized use. In other words, the rules of scope set precedence for encapsulation.

Something else which you need to know as a new beginner to Java programming is that you can have a nested scope. For you to understand this concept, study the code below:

```
// we are showing block scope
class ScopeShow {
int x; // this is accessible to all the code found in Main function
x = 12;
if (x == 12) {// we start a new scope
int y = 20; // only accessible to this block
// x and y are known here
System.out.println ("x and y: "+ X + ""+ y);
X = y* 2;
}
// y = 100; // an error is here, y is not known here, because it is found outside the
scope
// x is still visible here
System.out.println("x is "+ x);
}
}
```

The declaration of *x* happens at the start of the main method. This means that it is only visible to the part of code enclosed in the main method. Inside the if statement, we have the *y* variable declared. Given that a block will define the scope, *y* is accessible only to the part of the code inside the block. Again, inside the if block, we can use *x* because it is inside a nested scope.

One last point you should remember is variable are created when you enter the scope and ends when you exit scope. What this means is once we are out of the scope, the variable will not store its value.

Operators

Java has an extensive list of operator environment. If you are wondering what an operator is, you can look at it as a symbol which conveys a specific message to the compiler to carry out a logical or mathematical operation. In Java, you will interact with four classes of operators. The four classes include:

- Logical operator

- Bitwise operator

- Relational operator

- Arithmetic operator

22

Like other computer languages, Java has a defined list of additional operators to take care of certain specific scenarios.

Arithmetic operators

Arithmetic operators in Java include:

- + represents addition

- - represents subtraction

- * represents multiplication

- / represents division

- % represents modulus

- ++ represents increment

- -- represents decrement

Operators such as +, -, *, and / all perform the same function just like the rest of other languages.

Chapter 3

Java Program Control Statements

In Java, we have three types of program control statements. That includes the **selection** statements which consist of the *switch* and *if*; **iteration** statements contain the *do-while, while,* and *for* loops. The **statement jump** consists of the *return, break,* and *continue*. Besides the return statement, the remaining control statements you are going to learn more about here.

The if control statement

In the previous chapter, you have briefly interacted with the structure of an if statement. It takes the following construct:

if(condition) {

    //sequence statement

}

    else

    {

    //sequence statement

    }

This is one of the simplest forms of the if statement. It is straightforward to understand. At no point will all the sequence statements be executed at the same time. What you should realize in the above if statement is that the condition expression which controls the flow of the if statement has to produce a true or false value. True or false is a boolean type. We want to see how an if statement works in a program. Before we look at the program, you need to notice that this program requires one to input a character with their keyboard. The Java method for this is the *System.in.read()*.

Here's a program similar to the guessing letter game:

```
// we are showing block scope
class ScopeShow {
int x; // this is accessible to all the code found in Main function
x = 12;
if (x == 12) {// we start a new scope
int y = 20; // only accessible to this block
// x and y are known here
System.out.println ("x and y: "+ X + ""+ y);
X = y* 2;
}
// y = 100; // an error is here, y is not known here, because it is found outside the scope
// x is still visible here
System.out.println("x is "+ x);
}
}
```

In this program, the user is prompted to key in a character from the keyboard. Then the if statement will compare if the character entered is correct with the answer. A correct answer will result in a message shown on the screen. Otherwise, a different message is shown to the user to tell him or her they are wrong.

Nested ifs

We have previously looked at nested scopes; now we want to look at nested ifs. You will interact most of the time with a nested if. The greatest lesson to learn is nested ifs point to the block of code with the else.

25

Read the following example:

```
If( i ==10) {
If (j < 20) a = b;
If (k > 100) c = d;
else a – c; // this else will point to the if (k > 100)
}
else a = d; //this else will point to the if (i ==10)
|
```

You should be able to note that the last else has not been associated with if(j<20), but associated with the if(i==10).

if-else-if Ladder

This is a common programming syntax which depends on the nested if. It picks the following construct:

```
If(condition)

Statement

else if (condition)

statement

else if (condition)

statement

else

statement
```

In this syntax, the conditional expressions are tested from top to bottom. The moment a true condition is evaluated, the statement which is linked to it gets executed while the remaining sections are skipped. Supposing all conditions evaluated to be untrue, the last else statement runs. In this type of else statement, the final else is considered the

26

default condition. If you fail to include the final else, no action will happen.

This program shows the if-else-if ladder:

```
// Demonstrate an if-else-if ladder.
class Ladder {
  public static void main(String args[]) {
    int x;

    for(x=0; x<6; x++) {
      if(x==1)
        System.out.println("x is one");
      else if(x==2)
        System.out.println("x is two");
      else if(x==3)
        System.out.println("x is three");
      else if(x==4)
        System.out.println("x is four");
      else
        System.out.println("x is not between 1 and 4"); ←——— This is the
    }                                                          default statement.
  }
}
```

The program produces the following output:

```
x is not between 1 and 4
x is one
x is two
x is three
x is four
x is not between 1 and 4
```

From this program, you should be able to realize that *else* statement is only executed when there is no *if* statement which is true.

The Switch Statement

The next of Java's selection statement you will learn is the *switch*. The switch statement will allow a program to pick from various choices available. The switch involves testing an expression value with constants. If it matches any of the choices, the following statements associated with it are run. Switch uses the following syntax:

27

```
switch(expression) {
  case constant1:
    statement sequence
    break;
  case constant2:
    statement sequence
    break;
  case constant3:
    statement sequence
    break;
  .
  .
  .
  default:
    statement sequence
}
```

The *default* statement will be executed when none of the case constant match the expression. It is an optional choice.

Here is a program which illustrates the switch statement:

```
// Demonstrate the switch.
class SwitchDemo {
  public static void main(String args[]) {
    int i;

    for(i=0; i<10; i++)
      switch(i) {
        case 0:
          System.out.println("i is zero");
          break;
        case 1:
          System.out.println("i is one");
          break;
        case 2:
          System.out.println("i is two");
          break;
        case 3:
          System.out.println("i is three");
          break;
        case 4:
          System.out.println("i is four");
          break;
        default:
          System.out.println("i is five or more");
      }
  }
}
```

The output produced by this program is shown here:

```
i is zero
i is one
i is two
i is three
i is four
i is five or more
i is five or more
i is five or more
i is five or more
i is five or more
```

You can see in the above example that whenever the loop iterates, the statement linked to the case statement with it gets executed while the rest are skipped. If i is >= 5, we have no case statement to match that, so the default case has to be executed. The break statement is optional, but a lot of switch statements still use it.

Nested switch statements

The same way we have nested ifs, we can also have nested switch statements. You can see this example:

```
switch(ch1) {
   case 'A': System.out.println("This A is part of outer switch.");
      switch(ch2) {
        case 'A':
          System.out.println("This A is part of inner switch");
          break;
        case 'B': // ...
      } // end of inner switch
    break;
  case 'B': // ...
```

The for loop

Since the start of Chapter one, you have been making use of the *for* loop. You will be surprised to learn that the for loop is efficient and flexible. Here is the basic syntax for of a for loop:

for(*initialization; condition; iteration) statement;*

For repeating a block, the general form is

for(*initialization; condition; iteration)*
{
   statement sequence
}

The *condition* has a true or false expression which will define if the for loop can make another cycle. The iteration expression determines the number of times the loop repeats. Here you should see that we have separated all the three parts of the loop by semicolons.

The for loop will progress with the execution if the condition is always found to be true. If the condition is evaluated to be false, the program exits and executes the next line of code of the program.

This program below demonstrates the use of a for loop:
```
//1-99 and the rounding error
Class SqrRoot {
public static void main (String args []) {
double number, sroot,rerr;
for (number = 1.0; number < 100.0; number++) {
sroot = Math.sqrt(number);
System.out.println("Square root of "+ number + "is "+ sroot);
// compute the error
rerr = number – (sroot * sroot);
System.out.println("Rounding error is "+ rerr);
System.out.println();
}
}
}
```

You should realize that to compute the rounding error, we square the square root of every number. Later, subtract the outcome from the previous number.

The While loop

The general structure of a while loop includes:

while(condition) {

//sequence

}

In the while loop, the loop will repeat as long as the condition is true. A false condition will result in the program exiting the loop. To demonstrate the while loop, below is a program:

```
// while loop in java
class WhileDem {
public static void main (String args []) {
char ch;
// print using the while loop
ch = "b";
while (ch < = 'z') {
System.out.println(ch);
ch++;
}
}
}
```

In this example, we have initialized *ch* and assigned the value *"b"*. Every time the loop runs, *ch* is displayed then incremented. The process will proceed until the time we have the value of ch higher than *z*.

The do-while loop

It is the last type of loop in Java. When it comes to *do-while* loop, it is different compared to the while and for loops. The do-while loop will run the code inside it at least once before it tests the condition. Here is the syntax of a do-while loop:

do

{

statements;

}

While (condition);

Even though it is not important to have the braces, they are placed there to improve the readability so that we do not confuse it with the while loop. In this program, we implement with the do-while loop:

```
// Demonstrate the do-while loop.
class DWDemo {
  public static void main(String args[])
    throws java.io.IOException {

    char ch;

    do {
      System.out.print("Press a key followed by ENTER: ");
      ch = (char) System.in.read(); // get a char
    } while(ch != 'q');
  }
}
```

Break to exit a loop

Sometimes you might want to exit a loop even if it has not run to completion. You may have achieved what you wanted and you don't see the need to continue running the loop. This is the time when the *break* statement becomes important. A *break* statement placed in a loop forces the loop to terminate. This makes the program to resume executing the subsequent lines.

32

Look at this example:

```
// Using break to exit a loop.
class BreakDemo {
  public static void main(String args[]) {
    int num;

    num = 100;

    // loop while i-squared is less than num
    for(int i=0; i < num; i++) {
      if(i*i >= num) break; // terminate loop if i*i >= 100
      System.out.print(i + " ");
    }
    System.out.println("Loop complete.");
  }
}
```

This program generates the following output:

```
0 1 2 3 4 5 6 7 8 9 Loop complete.
```

The *break* statement in this example has been used to terminate the loop. The *break* statement can be freely applied in whichever type of loop in Java language.

The use of continue

While you can terminate the execution of a loop, it is also possible to skip the normal control structure of a loop. The *continue* statement will help you achieve this.

```
// Use continue.
class ContDemo {
  public static void main(String args[]) {
    int i;

    // print even numbers between 0 and 100
    for(i = 0; i<=100; i++) {
      if((i%2) != 0) continue; // iterate
      System.out.println(i);
    }
  }
}
```

Chapter 4

Starting Out with Classes in Java, Objects, and Methods

To become a professional Java programmer, you must understand the concept of classes in Java. The class is the main part of any Java program. In other words, it is the basis on which the whole Java language is created, and one reason for this is that the class holds the features of an object.

Inside a class, you will find data defined as well as the code which executes the data. The code exists in the methods. This chapter will take you through a brief understanding of the classes, methods, and objects in Java. It is crucial that you have a basic foundation of the above features so that you can know how to write complicated Java programs.

The fundamentals of Class

Since the start of this book, we have been using Java class. You should have noticed that every Java program has a class. Although we have been using Java classes, the classes were simple and we did not take advantage of the many features which a class comes with. Soon you will discover that the Java class is even more efficient than what we have used previously in the different programs.

So, let's start by looking at the basics of a class in Java. We can look at a class as a blueprint which determines the object properties. It defines in detail the program data and code. And so, a class is like a template which describes how you can create an object. It is vital to be elaborate about a class; it is a logical abstraction. Methods and variable of a class are referred to as members.

The basic style of a class

Whenever you describe a class, you will be declaring its nature and form. To declare a class involves making a specification of its instance variables as well as the methods of the class. While simple classes may only have methods or some might have instance variables alone, the majority of the real-world classes have both the class and instance variables.

The keyword class is used in declaring a class. Here is an easy class definition:

```
class classname {
    // declare instance variables
    type var1;
    type var2;
    // ...
    type varN;

    // declare methods
    type method1(parameters) {
        // body of method
    }

    type method2(parameters) {
        // body of method
    }
    // ...
    type methodN(parameters) {
        // body of method
    }
}
```

A class defined clearly should have a logical entity. For instance, if we have a class which holds telephone numbers and names of people, it will never hold other unrelated information such as average rainfall. The point to note here is that a class which is well-designed will store information that is logically connected. If you store information which is unrelated to the class, it will destroy the structure of your code.

So far, we have used classes which come with a single *main()* method. Soon you will learn how to build other methods, but I want you to know that the basic style of a class is not the way the *main()* method is defined.

We only need the *main()* method in case our class as it is the beginning point of our program. In addition, certain types of Java applications don't need the *main()* method.

Definition of a class

To reveal the concept of Java classes, we shall create a class which will store information about vehicles. The class is called *Vehicle*. This class will have information such as the number of passengers, the capacity of the fuel, as well as the average fuel consumption. In this class, we have three instance variables defined: fuel cap, passengers, and mpg. You should be keen to realize that the class Vehicle is without a method. At the moment, we consider it a data class.

```
class Vehicle {
  int passengers;  // number of passengers
  int fuelcap;     // fuel capacity in gallons
  int mpg;         // fuel consumption in miles per gallon
}
```

By defining a class, it has to create a new data type.

Don't forget that class declaration involves only specifying the type description. No actual object is created. Therefore, the previous example will not enforce the objects of type vehicle to become active.

This statement helps one create an object which belongs to the Vehicle class.

Vehicle minisalon = new Vehicle(); // we have created a variable object called minisalon

When this statement is executed, *minisalon* becomes an instance of the class *Vehicle*. Now, it will be said to have a physical reality. To access any member of a class, the dot operator helps you achieve that:

Object.Member

Take, for instance, we want our *minisalon* to hold the value 12. This is how it is done:

minisalon.fuelcap = 12;

Overall, the dot operator allows you to access the methods and instance variables. You can take a look at this entire program which uses the Vehicle class:

```
/* A program that uses the Vehicle class.

   Call this file VehicleDemo.java
*/
class Vehicle {
  int passengers; // number of passengers
  int fuelcap;    // fuel capacity in gallons
  int mpg;        // fuel consumption in miles per gallon
}
// This class declares an object of type Vehicle.
class VehicleDemo {
  public static void main(String args[]) {
    Vehicle minivan = new Vehicle();
    int range;

    // assign values to fields in minivan
    minivan.passengers = 7;
    minivan.fuelcap = 16;  ←————— Notice the use of the dot
    minivan.mpg = 21;            operator to access a member.

    // compute the range assuming a full tank of gas
    range = minivan.fuelcap * minivan.mpg;
    System.out.println("Minivan can carry " + minivan.passengers +
                       " with a range of " + range);
  }
}
```

If you want to run this program, you need to run the file with the name *Vehicle.Demo.java*. The main method is found in that class. This program will display:

```
Minivan can carry 7 with a range of 336
```

Reference variables and assignment

When handling the assignment operation in Java, you should underline that the object reference behaves differently from primitive variables. In this case, if you will assign a primitive type variable to another, it is simple. In simple terms, what the left variable does is to store what is held in the variable at right. However, if you choose that you will allot a single object reference variable to the other, the scenario becomes complicated. Why? You will be modifying the object which the reference variable refers to. Here is an example:

```
Vehicle car1 = new Vehicle ();
Vehicle car2 = car1;
```

By looking at the above code snippet, you might reason that both objects point to separate objects, however, that is not true. In this code, both car1 and car2 point to the same object. Something I would like you to learn here is that even though we have car1 and car2 pointing to the same object. They aren't related.

Methods

As we had said before, methods are members of the classes. At the moment, our Vehicle class has data, but no methods. While having a class which contains data alone is valid, the majority of the classes will have methods. Methods act upon the data which has been defined in the class, and most of the time it offers access to the data.

A method can carry at least one statement. A fully written Java code will contain a method which acts only on one particular task. Every method must be given a name. The name of the method helps one use the method in the code. You can choose to give your method whichever name you want, but note that the *main()* method is meant for the method which will start your program execution. Another important point is that you should never use Java keywords as part of your method name. The syntax for Java methods includes:

Type Your_methodname (parameter-list) {

//the body

}

In the above example, the *type* represents the type of data you would want your method to return. A *void* method is one which does not return data. We specify method name by *your_methodname*. The *parameter-list* refers to a series of type and identifier differentiated using commas. Parameters point to variables which are going to acquire the arguments which have been passed to the method after it has been called.

We give a method the Java vehicle class

To add a method to the Vehicle class, we will state it in the Vehicle's declaration. In this example, the Vehicle has a method called *range()* which output several types of vehicle:

```
// Add range to Vehicle.

class Vehicle {
  int passengers; // number of passengers
  int fuelcap;    // fuel capacity in gallons
  int mpg;        // fuel consumption in miles per gallon

  // Display the range.
  void range() {  ◄─────── The range() method is contained within the Vehicle class.
    System.out.println("Range is " + fuelcap * mpg);
  }                                      ▲         ▲
}                                        └────┬────┘
                    Notice that fuelcap and mpg are used directly, without the dot operator.

class AddMeth {
  public static void main(String args[]) {
    Vehicle minivan = new Vehicle();
    Vehicle sportscar = new Vehicle();

    int range1, range2;

    // assign values to fields in minivan
    minivan.passengers = 7;
    minivan.fuelcap = 16;
    minivan.mpg = 21;

    // assign values to fields in sportscar
    sportscar.passengers = 2;
    sportscar.fuelcap = 14;
    sportscar.mpg = 12;

    System.out.print("Minivan can carry " + minivan.passengers +
                     ". ");

    minivan.range(); // display range of minivan

    System.out.print("Sportscar can carry " + sportscar.passengers +
                     ". ");

    sportscar.range(); // display range of sportscar.
  }
}
```

This program will show the following output:

```
Minivan can carry 7. Range is 336
Sportscar can carry 2. Range is 168
```

40

We now want to review this program by starting with the method range(). Here is the first line:

Void range() {

What happens here is that we have declared a method whose name is *range*, and it has no parameter. The body of the method has the *System.out.println("......");* construct which will display the range of the vehicle after performing a few calculations. The method *range()* closes when it encounters the closing curly brace. This leads to the main program control to switch to the original caller. Well, let's review the code starting from the main method:

Minivan.range();

What is happening here is that the *range()* method is called by using the object variable minivan. Calling a program causes the program control to migrate to the method. And so, if the method execution comes to an end, control is relayed to the caller, and the program execution resumes from the following code. If we consider the above example, the method *range* here is going to display all the variation of vehicles defined by the minivan, similar to a call done by *sportscar*. Whenever you call *range()*, it will output the range listed by the object.

There is one particular thing you should discover about the method *range()*. Some of the instance variables have been addressed directly using the . operator.

Returning to a method

Generally, we have only two conditions which result in a method returning a value. First, the closing curly brace interacts with the method—this is clear in the method *range()*. The second condition for a method to return happens when a *return* statement gets executed. Don't forget that there are two types of return: the *void* method and the other one which returns values. We shall look at the first form here:

In a void method, it is possible to enforce an immediate termination by applying the *return* statement.

When the return statement is executed, the program control will get back to the caller by jumping all the rest of the code in a method. Consider the following example:

```
type-specifier array_name[ ] [ ] = {
    { val, val, val, ..., val },
    { val, val, val, ..., val },


    { val, val, val, ..., val }
};
```

In this case, the for loop will execute from 0–5 because when it reaches 5, the method is enforced to return a value. You can still develop many return statements in one Java method, especially when you have two pathways.

Returning a Value

While it is rare for a void method to return a value, there are specific methods which return a value. The potential for the method to have a return is an important property of a method. You have perhaps seen an example in the square root function to find the square root. Return value is important in programming to show a given result of a calculation like in the *sqrt()* function.

Sometimes, the return value proves the success or failure of a given method. The syntax used for a method with a return value is:

return *value;*

Chapter 5

In-depth look at Data types and Operators

In this chapter, we are going to discuss arrays, the bitwise operators, string types, and the ternary operator.

Arrays

We haven't covered anything about arrays in the previous chapter. However, what you should note is that arrays are simply a collection of variables of a similar type. Java arrays can take more than one form and dimension, even though you will discover that the one-dimension type of array is popular. Arrays are applied in programming to accomplish several tasks because they are the best for handling many related items.

The greatest benefit of arrays is that it arranges the data in a manner which is easy to modify. For instance, let's say you have an array which has the salary for different people. It becomes easy to calculate the total of the salary or even the average of the salary. Arrays will also organize the data in a manner which will make everything simple to sort.

While Java arrays can still be used the way we do in other languages, they have a unique feature: you implement them using objects. Implementing arrays as objects gives several advantages.

The one-dimensional arrays

When we talk about a one-dimensional array, we are referring to variables in a list that have a certain relation. These lists are very popular in the programming languages. A one-dimensional array is declared in the following way:

Type array-name [] = new type [size];

In this case, the type of array shows which type the array is while the number of items the array can hold is defined by the array size. When you implement arrays as objects, it has two procedures to adhere to. First, declare the array reference variable, then finalize by setting aside the memory for the array. You can look at this example:

Int team [] = new int [11];

As you can notice, array declaration will work the same way we do when you want to initialize an object. The *team* variable will store an address to the memory which has been assigned by *new*. However, for objects, we can break the above example into two:

int team [];

team = new int [11];

In the above example, when *team* is created, it has no physical object related to it, but when the following statement gets executed, *team* is associated with the array.

An index helps one access individual elements in an array. It specifies the correct position of each element stored in the array. Java arrays begin at 0. Since the array *team* has 11 elements, its index is from 0 to 10. If you want to perform array indexing, you must delineate every element which you want using square brackets. We use arrays in programming because they will help one handle a large number of associated variables. An example of a program which uses an array:

```
// Find the minimum and maximum values in an array.
class MinMax {
  public static void main(String args[]) {
    int nums[] = new int[10];
    int min, max;

    nums[0] = 99;
    nums[1] = -10;
    nums[2] = 100123;
    nums[3] = 18;
    nums[4] = -978;
    nums[5] = 5623;
    nums[6] = 463;
    nums[7] = -9;
    nums[8] = 287;
    nums[9] = 49;
    min = max = nums[0];
    for(int i=1; i < 10; i++) {
      if(nums[i] < min) min = nums[i];
      if(nums[i] > max) max = nums[i];
    }
    System.out.println("min and max: " + min + " " + max);
  }
}
```

The output from the program is shown here:

```
min and max: -978 100123
```

Two-dimensional array

This is among the easiest type of multidimensional array. You declare it as shown below:

Int table [] [] = new int [10] [30];

In this example, we have a two-dimensional array:

```
// Demonstrate a two-dimensional array.
class TwoD {
  public static void main(String args[]) {
    int t, i;
    int table[][] = new int[3][4];

    for(t=0; t < 3; ++t) {
      for(i=0; i < 4; ++i) {
        table[t][i] = (t*4)+i+1;
        System.out.print(table[t][i] + " ");
      }
      System.out.println();
    }
  }
}
```

45

Three or more dimensional arrays

Java still has arrays of more than two dimensions. Here is how it is declared:

type name[ ][ ]...[ ] = new *type*[*size1*][*size2*]...[*sizeN*];

How to initialize multi-dimensional arrays

To initialize a multi-dimensional array, you have to enclose every dimension using specific curly braces. For instance, the general style to apply when you want to initialize a two-dimensional array includes:

```
type-specifier array_name[ ][ ] = {
    { val, val, val, ..., val },
    { val, val, val, ..., val },
    -
    -
    -
    { val, val, val, ..., val }
};
```

In this example, *val* is the variable which is applied in the initialization. For each block inside the curly braces, it represents a specific row. For every row, it will hold the first value of the subarray. When we review the second value, it will take the second position, and the cycle continues. You must realize we are using commas to delineate the semicolon and the variable for initialization. The program below, the array *sqrs* is initialized with numbers between 1 to 10 together with their squares.

```
// Initialize a two-dimensional array.
class Squares {
  public static void main(String args[]) {
    int sqrs[][] = {
      { 1,  1 },
      { 2,  4 },
      { 3,  9 },
      { 4,  16 },
      { 5,  25 },          Notice how each row has
      { 6,  36 },          its own set of initializers.
      { 7,  49 },
      { 8,  64 },
      { 9,  81 },
      { 10, 100 }
    };
    int i, j;

    for(i=0; i < 10; i++) {
      for(j=0; j < 2; j++)
        System.out.print(sqrs[i][j] + " ");
      System.out.println();
    }
  }
}
```

Assigning array references

Similar to other objects, when you chose to earmark an array a reference variable to another, you will be shifting the object which the variable points to. You will not be leading to a copy of an array to make any changes to the details stored in the array.

You can consider this example:

47

```
// Assigning array reference variables.
class AssignARef {
  public static void main(String args[]) {
    int i;

    int nums1[] = new int[10];
    int nums2[] = new int[10];

    for(i=0; i < 10; i++)
      nums1[i] = i;

    for(i=0; i < 10; i++)
      nums2[i] = -i;
    System.out.print("Here is nums1: ");
    for(i=0; i < 10; i++)
      System.out.print(nums1[i] + " ");
    System.out.println();

    System.out.print("Here is nums2: ");
    for(i=0; i < 10; i++)
      System.out.print(nums2[i] + " ");
    System.out.println();

    nums2 = nums1; // now nums2 refers to nums1  ◄————Assign an array reference.

    System.out.print("Here is nums2 after assignment: ");
    for(i=0; i < 10; i++)
      System.out.print(nums2[i] + " ");
    System.out.println();

    // now operate on nums1 array through nums2
    nums2[3] = 99;

    System.out.print("Here is nums1 after change through nums2: ");
    for(i=0; i < 10; i++)
      System.out.print(nums1[i] + " ");
    System.out.println();
  }
}
```

The output from the program is shown here:

```
Here is nums1: 0 1 2 3 4 5 6 7 8 9
Here is nums2: 0 -1 -2 -3 -4 -5 -6 -7 -8 -9
Here is nums2 after assignment: 0 1 2 3 4 5 6 7 8 9
Here is nums1 after change through nums2: 0 1 2 99 4 5 6 7 8 9
```

The for-each loop

Sometimes situations arise in dealing with arrays where it is a requirement to go through every element in the array. Such situations are many, like if you want to perform an average operation or do a sum calculation. You will have to add every value stored in the array. The procedure of individually adding each element before you can perform the average is tiresome.

This type of for loop we will discuss is *for-each*. A for loop will go around a collection of objects in a sequential style from the start to the end. The general syntax of a for-each loop is:

for(*type itr-var : collection*) *statement-block*

Strings

String is also another crucial element of the Java data type. A string will define and support the character string. In many programming languages, a string is an array of characters. But, Java is a bit different. Instead, strings are considered objects.

For your information, we have used the string class from the time this book started, but you never realized that. Any time you decide to declare a string literal, you will simply be creating an object of String. For instance, the statement:

System.out.println("Strings are objects in Java");

"Strings are objects in Java" is automatically defined into a string object by Java.

Constructing a string

To declare a string, you do it the same way you can declare other objects:

String play = new String ("how are you");

This code will generate a String object called *play* which has the character string *"how are you"*. It is still possible to generate a string with the help of a different String. Take this example:

String play = new String ("How are you");
String play1 = new String (play);

When the code executes, play1 will also contain the string "How are you".

What you need to know is that the moment you create your string object, you can really make use of it any place where quoted strings are permitted. For instance, you may use it in *println()*, this is provided in the example below:

```
// Introduce String.
class StringDemo {
  public static void main(String args[]) {
    // declare strings in various ways
    String str1 = new String("Java strings are objects.");
    String str2 = "They are constructed various ways.";
    String str3 = new String(str2);

    System.out.println(str1);
    System.out.println(str2);
    System.out.println(str3);
  }
}
```

The output from the program is shown here:

```
Java strings are objects.
They are constructed various ways.
They are constructed various ways.
```

How to operate on Strings

The class string has different methods which work on strings. You can look at them in the table below:

boolean equals(str)	Returns true if the invoking string contains the same character sequence as str.
int length( )	Obtains the length of a string.
char charAt(index)	Obtains the character at the index specified by index.
int compareTo(str)	Returns less than zero if the invoking string is less than str, greater than zero if the invoking string is greater than str, and zero if the strings are equal.
int indexOf(str)	Searches the invoking string for the substring specified by str. Returns the index of the first match or −1 on failure.
int lastIndexOf(str)	Searches the invoking string for the substring specified by str. Returns the index of the last match or −1 on failure.

If you would like to see a program which uses the above methods. Here is an example

```
// Some String operations.
class StrOps {
  public static void main(String args[]) {
    String str1 =
      "When it comes to Web programming, Java is #1.";
    String str2 = new String(str1);
    String str3 = "Java strings are powerful.";
    int result, idx;
    char ch;

    System.out.println("Length of str1: " +
                       str1.length());

    // display str1, one char at a time.
    for(int i=0; i < str1.length(); i++)
      System.out.print(str1.charAt(i));
    System.out.println();
    if(str1.equals(str2))
      System.out.println("str1 equals str2");
    else
      System.out.println("str1 does not equal str2");

    if(str1.equals(str3))
      System.out.println("str1 equals str3");
    else
      System.out.println("str1 does not equal str3");

    result = str1.compareTo(str3);
    if(result == 0)
      System.out.println("str1 and str3 are equal");
    else if(result < 0)
      System.out.println("str1 is less than str3");
    else
      System.out.println("str1 is greater than str3");

    // assign a new string to str2
    str2 = "One Two Three One";

    idx = str2.indexOf("One");
    System.out.println("Index of first occurrence of One: " + idx);
    idx = str2.lastIndexOf("One");
    System.out.println("Index of last occurrence of One: " + idx);
  }
}
```

This program generates the following output:

```
Length of str1: 45
When it comes to Web programming, Java is #1.
str1 equals str2
str1 does not equal str3
str1 is greater than str3
Index of first occurrence of One: 0
Index of last occurrence of One: 14
```

Just like any other data type, it is possible to assemble strings like arrays. For instance:

```
// Demonstrate String arrays.
class StringArrays {
  public static void main(String args[]) {
    String strs[] = { "This", "is", "a", "test." };

    System.out.println("Original array: ");
    for(String s : strs)
      System.out.print(s + " ");
    System.out.println("\n");

    // change a string
    strs[1] = "was";
    strs[3] = "test, too!";

    System.out.println("Modified array: ");
    for(String s : strs)
      System.out.print(s + " ");
  }
}
```

"Strings are immutable"

What this means is that once you have the strings created, you can't modify the character sequence of the string. This type of limit permits Java to implement strings in an efficient way. While this might sound like a big disadvantage, it is not. If you want a string which is a modification of the one you already have, just create the string which has the desired modifications.

52

Use a string to control the switch statement

In the previous chapter, we saw that the switch control statement had to be an integer type like *char* or *int*. Today, we can apply a string as the control of a switch. This will lead to a code which is readable and efficient in most situations.

This example will illustrate how to control a switch with a String.

```
// Use a string to control a switch statement.

class StringSwitch {
  public static void main(String args[]) {

    String command = "cancel";

    switch(command) {
      case "connect":
        System.out.println("Connecting");
        break;
      case "cancel":
        System.out.println("Canceling");
        break;
      case "disconnect":
        System.out.println("Disconnecting");
        break;
      default:
        System.out.println("Command Error!");
        break;
    }
  }
}
```

This program will display the output: Cancelling

Bitwise Operators

While in the opening chapters we learned the logical, relational and arithmetic operators, Java still has other operators which cover different types of problems. These are the bitwise operators. You can use the bitwise operators on *short, long, byte* or *int* values. However, we can't apply operations of this type of operator on *float, double* and *boolean* or even class types. We call them bitwise operators because of

53

their operation: they alter the bits that produce a value. This table shows some of the bitwise operators:

Operator	Result
&	Bitwise AND
|	Bitwise OR
^	Bitwise exclusive OR
>>	Shift right
>>>	Unsigned shift right
<<	Shift left
~	One's complement (unary NOT)

The ? Operator

This is the most interesting thing about Java operators. Often, the ? Replaces most used if-else:

```
I
If(condition)
Var = expression1;
Else
Var = expression2;
```

The ? is the ternary operator. Its syntax is:

Exp1? Exp2: Exp3:

The first expression is the Boolean type, while the second and third expression can be any type of expression. Make sure you note the placement of the colon.

This is how the ternary works: exp1 is tested, then if true, exp2 is taken to be the value of the whole expression tested. However, when it happens that exp1 is not true, exp3 will automatically be the current value of the expression.

Below is an example of the ? operator:

```
// Prevent a division by zero using the ?.
class NoZeroDiv {
  public static void main(String args[]) {
  int result;

  for(int i = -5; i < 6; i++) {
    result = i != 0 ? 100 / i : 0;  ◄──────── This prevents a divide-by-zero.
    if(i != 0)
      System.out.println("100 / " + i + " is " + result);
    }
  }
}
```

The output from the program is shown here:

```
100 / -5 is -20
100 / -4 is -25
100 / -3 is -33
100 / -2 is -50
100 / -1 is -100
100 / 1 is 100
100 / 2 is 50
100 / 3 is 33
100 / 4 is 25
100 / 5 is 20
```

Chapter 6

Inheritance in Java

This chapter will proceed with the objected-oriented programming in Java. In this chapter, we discuss inheritance in Java. Inheritance is another way of software reuse. It involves creating a new software by making use of existing class members. Inheritance will allow you to save time during the process of program development by creating new classes on existing classes. Inheritance further provides for the chance that a system will be developed and maintained effectively.

An existing class in Java is called the superclass while a new class declared is called the subclass. In the C++ programming language, the superclass is the base class while the subclass is the derived class. Every subclass may become a superclass for the later subclasses.

A subclass can later create its own methods and classes. This means a subclass is specific compared to the superclass and it represents a specialized group of objects.

In Java, the class inheritance will start with the class object. Java has only single inheritance. This is where each class is extracted from one direct superclass.

Superclass and Subclasses

Usually, an object which belongs to one class is an object of another class too. You can take a look at the superclasses and subclasses below:

Superclass	Subclasses
Student	GraduateStudent, UndergraduateStudent
Shape	Circle, Triangle, Rectangle, Sphere, Cube
Loan	CarLoan, HomeImprovementLoan, MortgageLoan
Employee	Faculty, Staff
BankAccount	CheckingAccount, SavingsAccount

Taking one example above, we can say CheckingAccount inherits from the class BankAccount. In other words, CheckingAccount is a subclass and BankAccount is the class. Since each subclass belongs to a superclass, and it is possible to have a single superclass with many subclasses, we can say that a superclass represents a large set of objects compared to what a subclass can represent. For instance, the superclass shape will represent all types of shapes, but the subclass circle will represent specific types of circles.

Member hierarchy in a university community

The inheritance relationship builds a specific tree-like structure. The superclass at the top while the subclass comes below the superclass. We want to build an inheritance hierarchy of a university community. You know well that a university has thousands of people including students, alumni, professors, and employees. The employees can still be for the staff or faculty members. The faculty members can further be administrators such as chairpersons or lecturers. The hierarchy could have a lot of classes. For instance, we can have students who are undergraduate and graduate. The undergraduates can further be categorized into freshmen, juniors, sophomores, and seniors.

Every arrow in the above hierarchy indicates an is-a relationship.

The shape hierarchy

Let's now look at the shape hierarchy. This hierarchy will start with a super-class *Shape*. The superclass *Shape* is extended by *ThreeDimensionalShape* and *TwoDimensionalShape*. The third level in the shape hierarchy has specific types of *TwoDimensionalShape* as well as *ThreeDimensionalShape*. The same way we did for the University hierarchy, we can apply the same in the shape hierarchy. Find out how many relationships do we have. This shape hierarchy could have as many classes as possible.

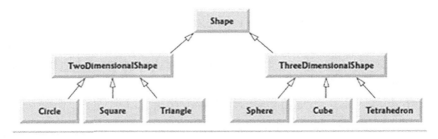

Something which you need to note is that not every class relationship can be an inheritance relationship.

Protected Members

At one point in this book, we discussed briefly the *public* and *private* modifiers. Public members are free to be accessed at any time but not the same case as protected members.

Now we want to look at an example:

We know that Java will support inheritance by providing for inclusion of one class into another one in the declaration. You achieve this with the keyword *extends*. Therefore, the subclass will extend to the superclass. Here is an example which demonstrates some dominant features of inheritance as discussed previously. The superclass in this program is *TwoDShape*. It holds both the dimensions of a 2-D object and a subclass referred to as *Triangle*. You should note the way the keyword *extends* has been used to develop the subclass.

```
// A simple class hierarchy.

// A class for two-dimensional objects.
class TwoDShape {
```

```java
  double width;
  double height;

  void showDim() {
    System.out.println("Width and height are " +
                       width + " and " + height);
  }
}

// A subclass of TwoDShape for triangles.
class Triangle extends TwoDShape {    // Triangle inherits TwoDShape.
  String style;

  double area() {
    return width * height / 2;    // Triangle can refer to the members of TwoDShape
  }                               //   as if they were part of Triangle.

  void showStyle() {
    System.out.println("Triangle is " + style);
  }
}

class Shapes {
  public static void main(String args[]) {
    Triangle t1 = new Triangle();
    Triangle t2 = new Triangle();

    t1.width = 4.0;
    t1.height = 4.0;    // All members of Triangle are available to Triangle
    t1.style = "filled";    //   objects, even those inherited from TwoDShape.

    t2.width = 8.0;
    t2.height = 12.0;
    t2.style = "outlined";

    System.out.println("Info for t1: ");
    t1.showStyle();
    t1.showDim();
    System.out.println("Area is " + t1.area());

    System.out.println();

    System.out.println("Info for t2: ");
    t2.showStyle();
    t2.showDim();
    System.out.println("Area is " + t2.area());
  }
}
```

The output of the above program is:

```
Info for t1:
Triangle is filled
Width and height are 4.0 and 4.0
Area is 8.0

Info for t2:
Triangle is outlined
Width and height are 8.0 and 12.0
Area is 48.0
```

In the above program, *TwoDShape* describes the features of the common two-dimensional shape. The class *Triangle* will create a precise category for a triangle in the *TwoDShape* class. The style of the triangle is kept in the style which can also have any string which defines more about the triangle. The method *area()* will calculate triangle area, while *showStyle()* output the shape of the triangle.

While *TwoDShape* is a superclass of the *Triangle*, it is still an independent class. Since it is a superclass for the subclass, that does not nullify it from getting used by its own. For instance, this is accepted:

```
TwoDShape shape = new TwoDShape ();
shape. width = 10;
shape. height = 30;
shape. showDim ();
```

The general nature of a class declaration takes a superclass like the way is indicated here:

```
class subclass-name extends superclass-name {
  // body of class
}
```

In Java, only a single superclass is permitted for a single subclass. This means you can't have multiple superclass inheritance.

Constructors and inheritance

In the hierarchy, we can have the superclass and subclasses having their own constructors. This brings up a very crucial issue on the role of a constructor in developing an object and subclass. Do we go with the one in the superclass or subclass? However, if you have experienced this problem, this is what you need to learn today: a superclass's constructor will have its own object, and the subclass's constructor will also have its own object. In the previous example, we have depended upon the default constructor built by Java. Now, this wasn't a problem. But, in the majority of the Java inheritance examples, there will be an explicit constructor. For instance, below is a modified example of the *Triangle* which defines the constructor:

```java
// Add a constructor to Triangle.

// A class for two-dimensional objects.
class TwoDShape {
  private double width; // these are
  private double height; // now private

  // Accessor methods for width and height.
  double getWidth() { return width; }
  double getHeight() { return height; }
  void setWidth(double w) { width = w; }
  void setHeight(double h) { height = h; }

  void showDim() {
    System.out.println("Width and height are " +
                       width + " and " + height);
  }
}
```

```
// A subclass of TwoDShape for triangles.
class Triangle extends TwoDShape {
  private String style;

  // Constructor
  Triangle(String s, double w, double h) {
    setWidth(w);
    setHeight(h);                                    ──── Initialize TwoDShape
                                                          portion of object.
    style = s;
  }

  double area() {
    return getWidth() * getHeight() / 2;
  }

  void showStyle() {
    System.out.println("Triangle is " + style);
  }
}

class Shapes3 {
  public static void main(String args[]) {
    Triangle t1 = new Triangle("filled", 4.0, 4.0);
    Triangle t2 = new Triangle("outlined", 8.0, 12.0);

    System.out.println("Info for t1: ");
    t1.showStyle();
    t1.showDim();
    System.out.println("Area is " + t1.area());

    System.out.println();

    System.out.println();

    System.out.println("Info for t2: ");
    t2.showStyle();
    t2.showDim();
    System.out.println("Area is " + t2.area());
  }
}
```

In this example, the *Triangle* constructor will initialize the members of the TwoDClass which have its own field. When we have both the "superclass and subclass" describe a constructor, the situation is much difficult since the all the superclass and subclass have to be executed. In such a scenario, you need to use the Java *super* keyword which takes two forms:

- Superclass constructor

- Access member of the superclass

Super calling the Superclass Constructors

It is possible for, let's say a subclass, to make a call to a constructor which is well-defined by the superclass. This is how it is defined:

super(parameter-list);

In the above syntax, the *parameter-list* refers to the parameters required by the constructor in the superclass. If you want to see how you can use *super()*, here is an example for you:

```
// Add constructors to TwoDShape.
class TwoDShape {
  private double width;
  private double height;

  // Parameterized constructor.
  TwoDShape(double w, double h) {  ◄———— A constructor for TwoDShape
    width = w;
    height = h;
  }

  // Accessor methods for width and height.
  double getWidth() { return width; }
  double getHeight() { return height; }
  void setWidth(double w) { width = w; }
  void setHeight(double h) { height = h; }

  void showDim() {
    System.out.println("Width and height are " +
                       width + " and " + height);
  }
}

// A subclass of TwoDShape for triangles.
class Triangle extends TwoDShape {
  private String style;

  Triangle(String s, double w, double h) {
    super(w, h); // call superclass constructor

    style = s;
  }
                                    Use super() to execute the
}                                   TwoDShape constructor.
```

64

```java
    double area() {
      return getWidth() * getHeight() / 2;
    }

    void showStyle() {
      System.out.println("Triangle is " + style);
    }
}

class Shapes4 {
  public static void main(String args[]) {
    Triangle t1 = new Triangle("filled", 4.0, 4.0);
    Triangle t2 = new Triangle("outlined", 8.0, 12.0);

    System.out.println("Info for t1: ");
    t1.showStyle();
    t1.showDim();
    System.out.println("Area is " + t1.area());

    System.out.println();

    System.out.println("Info for t2: ");
    t2.showStyle();
    t2.showDim();
    System.out.println("Area is " + t2.area());
  }
}
```

In this code, the *Triangle()* method will call the *super()* together with its parameters. This will result in the *TwoDShape()* constructor getting called. It then assigns the *height* and *width*. The *Triangle* will no longer initialize the above values by itself. This would make *TwoDShape* build its own smaller object in whichever way it selects. In addition, *TwoDShape* can extend the number of operations to be performed on the subclasses of which we have no knowledge. This prevents the current program from failing.

Overriding a method

Calling a method overridden inside a subclass will refer to the type of the method declared in the subclass.

```
// Method overriding.
class A {
  int i, j;
  A(int a, int b) {
    i = a;
    j = b;
  }

  // display i and j
  void show() {
    System.out.println("i and j: " + i + " " + j);
  }
}

class B extends A {
  int k;

  B(int a, int b, int c) {
    super(a, b);
    k = c;
  }

  // display k - this overrides show() in A
  void show() {  ◄──────────────────── This show() in B overrides
    System.out.println("k: " + k);        the one defined by A.
  }
}

class Override {
  public static void main(String args[]) {
    B subOb = new B(1, 2, 3);

    subOb.show(); // this calls show() in B
  }
}
```

The output:

> *K: 3*

When you call *show()* on type *B* object, the method *show()* declared
inside *B* is executed. This means this method *show()* within the B will
override the one stated in *A*.

Tips while starting out in Java

If you want to have a successful career in Java programming, perhaps
these tips will help you. They will help you attain your goals in
programming. You can apply them still in any other programming
language.

Master the basics

The basics of any language are important in helping you master the rest of the language. This book has given you the basics which can drive you to become a pro in Java. You can begin right away and read this book then master the highlighted basics of this language. It will help you begin your Java programming career at a much better level. Like all other things, if you are a complete beginner, you might look at code and think as if is a collection of letters and numbers. Just note that everyone started at that point. If you can withstand it, your future is going to be bright.

Practice to program frequently

Have you heard of the old cliché, "practice makes perfect?" Yes! It still applies in programming. If you are not ready to put in your sweat to learn the basics and the syntax of the language, you will not become the best or even a pro in Java. The best thing you have for you is that it is possible to practice coding wherever you are as long as you have a laptop. Once you get competent with the basics of the language, make it a hobby to spend most of your time trying to code in Java as well as understanding the different concepts of the language.

Set algorithm

This is where you put yourself in a trial test. You can't set your algorithm if you don't know the basics of the language. You will need to look for a problem or even create a problem for yourself and provide a solution for it. This is one of the steps in the learning curve. If you can solve as many questions as you can, the better you will become. Algorithms will play an important role in your entire life as a programmer because they direct your computer to know exactly what to do to solve a given problem. Before you can set your own algorithm, it is important to have some trials.

Look for more sources in Java

Best Java developers don't read one book about Java. Instead, they have as many books on their shelf to read about it. You need to pump your head with enough knowledge in Java so that you can easily know how to code and improve your problem-solving skills. Remember, most resources of Java are available online. You can spare time to browse the internet and find the recent information about the language. Regardless of your level of experience in Java, reading extra sources will be invaluable. I will still recommend that you become a member of an active forum online. Forums have people who ask questions in a given topic then experts come in and give a response. Quora could be a wonderful place to start, but there are still many forums which you can join.

Try and trace your code on paper

Do you know what that means? It would be great for you if you are just beginning.

Don't be afraid to request help when you need

This is the reason why it is important to join an online forum. If you know an answer to a solution, provide the answer. The best way to learn is to teach someone who does not know. It will help you master the concept and even understand it on a deeper level.

Stick to one kind of task

As a beginner in Java, you don't want to switch from one area to another. Remember, Java programming fits in many fields. You can focus on web programming with Java or create desktop applications in Java. Stick to one particular area so that you don't end up getting confused in the process.

Conclusion

Thank for making it through to the end of *Java: Basic Fundamental Guide for Beginners*. Let's hope it was informative and able to provide you with all of the tools you need to achieve your goals whatever they may be.

This book has taken you through the core fundamentals of Java to help you develop the right foundation to explore deeper concepts in Java. It is important for you to understand the various data types in Java: the variables, strings, and arrays. In addition, mastering the method, classes, and inheritance is crucial. Remember. Java is an object-oriented language. This means that having a deep understanding of the topic of classes, methods, and inheritance is fundamental.

Java is a very powerful language, it powers the majority of enterprises and organizations. It is one of the best languages for developers when they want to implement internet-based applications. Furthermore, software devices which must cross communicate over a given network are developed with the help of Java. Many devices today use Java. This shows how Java is an important computer programming language. While this book has tried to present you with the basics skills of programming in Java, it is highly important to emphasize that it is just a starting point. Java goes beyond the elements which determine the language. For you to become an excellent Java programmer, you need to take time to read deep and master the concepts in Java. Luckily, this book helps you develop the right knowledge to expand more on other areas of Java. Therefore, the next step for you to take after reading this book is to look for a comprehensive Java textbook to read.

Finally, if you found this book useful in any way, a review on Amazon is always appreciated!

Made in United States
North Haven, CT
14 November 2022

26724782R00046